START-A-CRAFT

Decoupage

Get started in a new craft with easy-to-follow
projects for beginners

LESLEY PLAYER

CHARTWELL
BOOKS, INC.

A QUINTET BOOK

Published by Chartwell Books
A Division of Book Sales, Inc.
114 Northfield Avenue
Edison, New Jersey 08837

This edition produced for sale
in the U.S.A., its territories
and dependencies only.

ISBN 0-7858-0572-9

This book was designed and produced by
Quintet Publishing Limited
6 Blundell Street
London N7 9BH

Creative Director: Richard Dewing
Designer: Bruce Low
Project Editor: Diana Steedman
Editor: Lydia Darbyshire
Photographer: Paul Forrester

Typeset in Great Britain by
Central Southern Typesetters, Eastbourne
Manufactured in Singapore by Eray Scan Pte Ltd
Printed in China by Leefung-Asco Printers Ltd

CONTENTS

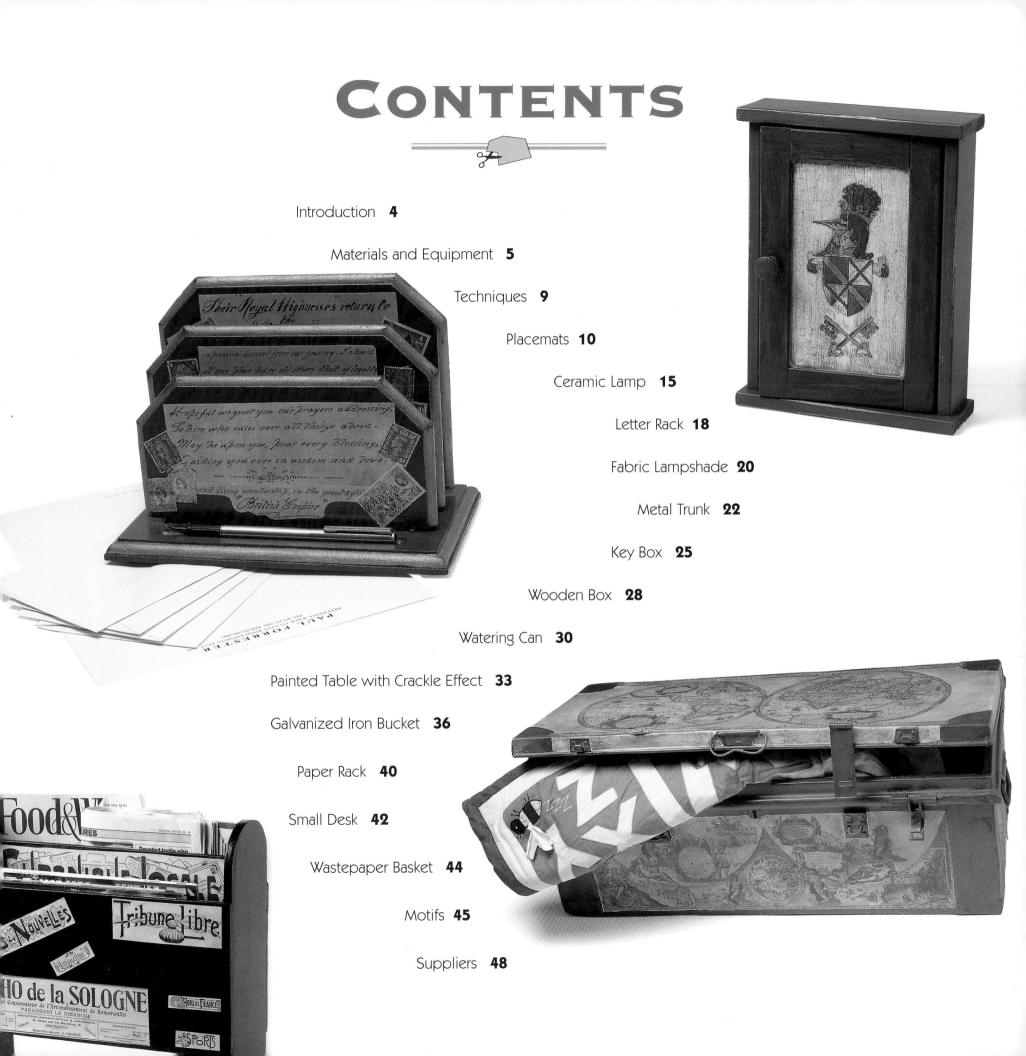

INTRODUCTION

The fascination of decoupage lies in its ability to transform old items of battered furniture or uninteresting household articles into attractive and eye-catching pieces that will enhance any room. Once you have been captured by the potential of the technique, you will want to try it on almost everything in your home. Every thrift shop, yard sale and garage sale will seem like an Aladdin's cave, brimming with articles ready for you to practice your skill. The joy of decoupage is that it enables you to decorate objects in such a variety of ways that you can personalize them for yourself and to suit your own home or in the styles that your family and friends like best.

Whenever we visit craft fairs and craft stores, we see the treasures that people have made from everyday objects. The purpose of this book is to show how easy it is to take the first steps on the way to being able to effect these transformations yourself.

Provided that the surfaces are correctly prepared, decoupage can be used on metal, wood, terracotta and pottery, glass, plastic, and cardboard. As you experiment, you will find that different approaches and techniques can be applied to achieve a variety of results, so that whether you are renovating an old piece or simply decorating an everyday object such as a wastepaper basket or plant pot, you will be able to adapt the basic methods to suit your own purposes.

Always make sure that something is worth rejuvenating before you begin. Decoupage can give worn and rusty pieces a new lease of life, but if you do not like the underlying shape or proportions of an item, no amount of hard work will change these or create an attractive object from something that is inherently unappealing.

There is hardly anything that cannot be wholly transformed by this basically easy craft. Experiment on simple objects to begin with and follow the guidelines explained on these pages, and you will soon be able to give a new life and personal style to every kind of household object.

MATERIALS AND EQUIPMENT

The materials and equipment needed for decoupage could hardly be simpler, and, apart from the actual illustrations you will use, you will probably already have many of them in your home tool box.

MOTIFS AND PICTURE SOURCES

It can be great fun collecting suitable pictures to use. Some of the illustrations used in the projects in this book appear on pages 45-47 to help you get started, but as your skill and interest in decoupage grows, you will begin to regard all kinds of printed material in a new light.

The recent revival in interest in the craft has meant that there are several books available that reprint interesting and amusing Victorian illustrations, which can be photocopied and colored. You will also find that gift-wrapping paper is a wonderful source of motifs, as are greetings cards. You can photocopy photographs, old prints, sheet music, letters, and stamps, which can be made to look as if they are antique by a simple aging process. Even magazines and newspapers contain illustrations that can be used – look out for fashion and computer magazines, which often contain stunning and colorful pictures. Old books, which turn up at garage sales and in thrift shops, can be an unexpected source of illustrations – old history books, for example, often contain interesting maps.

If you are using modern magazines, greeting cards, or gift-wrapping paper you can, of course, simply cut out the motifs you want. It is, however, probably better to photocopy illustrations from books, and most libraries and many stationery stores now have photocopiers, many of which have enlargement and reduction facilities. The great advantage of photocopying is that you can repeat a motif as often as you wish, and you can also photocopy onto colored or textured paper. Color photocopying is more expensive, and although there may be occasions when you prefer to have a

TIP
• Try not to use original source pictures because you will not be able to repeat a successful design. Most libraries and stationers have photocopying facilities, and coloring black and white copies is part of the pleasure of decoupage. Remember always to make the photocopies from the original for the best results.

colored copy, it is certainly less expensive and often more satisfying to hand-tint a black and white photocopy.

CUTTING EQUIPMENT

You will need a large pair of scissors for general cutting out, a smaller pair for cutting out motifs from gift-wrapping paper or magazines, and a pair of nail scissors for cutting out intricate shapes.

A craft knife or scalpel can be useful, especially if you have to cut out especially delicate shapes. Remember to work on a cutting mat. The special rubberized mats that are sold in craft stores are best because they are not damaged by score lines. Kitchen chopping boards can be used, but the best kinds will quickly blunt your blades while the cheaper kinds will eventually become marked. Kitchen boards are useful when you apply adhesive, however, because they are easily wiped clean.

SEALANTS

Paper must be sealed before it can be used for decoupage in order to prevent it from absorbing paint or varnish, to stop discoloration, and to inhibit colors from running. In addition, when a water-based adhesive such as white glue is used with paper, the paper tends to stretch when it is applied to a surface, causing wrinkles and air bubbles. Sealing the paper beforehand helps prevent this.

I prefer to use a sanding sealer or button polish, which I apply to both sides of the image. This gives the paper a slightly crisp feel, and it makes intricate cutting out easier. If you want an aged or antique look, use shellac, which is honey-colored.

Sanding sealer, button polish, and shellac are available from most hardware stores and from many craft and art stores. They are all alcohol based and dry quickly.

You can also use spray fixatives, water-based varnishes, or white craft glue, which should be diluted to the consistency of paint. Again, coat both sides of the image, and remember that water-based preparations take longer to dry than alcohol-based ones.

ADHESIVES

All the projects illustrated in this book were decorated with motifs glued with white craft glue. This water-based adhesive is white or yellow when it is wet and transparent when it is dry. It can be thinned with water and used as a varnish. When it is dry it has a hard, "plastic " feel. When you use it to apply individual motifs, always wipe away any excess adhesive from around the edge of the design with a damp cloth. White glue is available in craft and art stores and in hardware and stationery stores.

PAINTS

Water-based latex and acrylic paints are easy to use because they dry reasonably quickly and you can wash the brushes in water and detergent. (If you wish, use a hairdryer to speed up drying times.) The projects in this book were painted with flat latex paint.

Artists' paints can be used to color or decorate objects. Acrylic paints, which can be bought in tubes, cannot be used to bring out the cracks in a crackle varnish, however, because they are water-

based and the paint will adhere to the second coat of crackle varnish, which is also water-based, and will smudge when you try to wipe it off. You can use artists' acrylic paints to tint white latex paint both to create a background color or add lines and details to finished objects.

Artists' oil paints are used in an antique glaze or to bring out the cracks when crackle varnish is used. The paint is applied by dampening a cloth

with mineral spirits, squeezing a small amount of paint onto the cloth and rubbing it over the surface of the decoupaged item once the second-stage varnish is dry and the cracks have appeared. Raw umber is often used to enhance the cracks after the second stage of crackle varnish, while burnt umber creates reddish-brown cracks.

PRIMERS AND UNDERCOATS

Use a red oxide metal primer on metal. Clean your brushes in mineral spirits.

If you are decorating untreated wood, use acrylic primer followed by white acrylic undercoat.

VARNISHES AND FINISHES

When you have glued the motifs and the adhesive is absolutely dry, you must apply several layers of varnish. The aim is to "lose" the edges of the motifs in the varnish, and some people apply up to twenty coats, while others find that three or four coats are sufficient. However many coats you apply, you should leave each one to dry thoroughly, then sand it very lightly with the finest-grit sandpaper before applying the next. Do not sand the final coat. Make sure that you remove any dust adhering to the surface of the object before applying varnish.

The kind of varnish you will use will be largely determined by the use to which the object will be put. Trays and table mats, for example, will need a tough, heat-resistant, gloss surface that can be wiped clean. A lamp, on the other hand, will look

attractive if the light reflects from a smooth satin finish, and some pieces of furniture need a wax polish over a flat varnish. If you do not like your first choice and if you have not applied a wax polish, you can sand the surface gently with fine sandpaper and apply a varnish with a different finish.

As we have already noted, white glue can be diluted and used as a varnish. There are, however, several other kinds of varnish that you might prefer to use.

ACRYLIC VARNISH

This water-based varnish is especially easy to use. You can wash your brushes in water; it does not have a strong, pungent smell; it dries fairly quickly; it is waterproof when it is dry; and it does not yellow with age. Acrylic varnish can be bought in hardware and do-it-yourself stores and in art stores, and it is available in flat, gloss, and silk finishes.

WATER-BASED VARNISH

A water-based varnish takes only 10–15 minutes to dry, making it especially useful when you are trying to build up several layers to blur the edges of your cut-out motifs as quickly as possible. It is available from good art stores in gloss, flat, and satin finishes. I use it because it dries so quickly.

POLYURETHANE VARNISH

Polyurethane wood varnish is available in all hardware stores, and it comes in flat, gloss, and satin finishes and in a range of tints, including clear. It does have a tendency to yellow slightly with age, and so it can be used when you want to give an "aged" effect to your work. Many people prefer polyurethane varnish to acrylic varnish, which has a rather hard appearance.

SHELLAC

You can use shellac to seal most surfaces, including paper and new wood, but it is not heat-resistant and you must apply a coat of varnish to finish off. Shellac is honey-colored and is often used to "age" pieces. It is also useful as an insulating layer between two incompatible paints or varnishes. Clean your brushes in denatured alcohol.

WHITE POLISH

Like shellac, of which it is a rather more refined version, white polish is alcohol-based. It gives a transparent finish that will dissolve in denatured alcohol, even when it is dry. Use it when you do not want an antique effect.

CRACKLE VARNISH

Also sometimes known as cracklure, crackle varnish is sold in a two-stage pack in art and craft stores. The first coat is oil-based, and it continues to dry under the second, faster drying, water-based layer, which causes the top coat to crack. It is a fascinating varnish to use because the results are always unpredictable.

Drying times vary, depending on the thickness of the varnish and on the temperature and humidity of the room in which it is applied. You can speed up the second stage by using a hairdryer, set to medium, held about 2 feet away from the surface. When it is dry, the cracked varnish can be aged with artists' oil paints to reveal the cracks to best effect. If you do not like the results, you can wash off the second coat and try again.

You can buy a wholly water-based crackle varnish, which is available in some craft stores. It is simpler to use and gives more predictable results than oil-based cracklure. You can choose from a variety of "cracking" effects and sizes, which do not depend on temperature or humidity, and you may want to experiment with this type of crackle varnish until you feel confident enough to tackle the oil-based version.

Because new kinds of crackle varnish keep coming onto the market, make sure that you read the manufacturer's instructions before you begin. If

Crackle varnish–first, oil-based coat

Crackle varnish – second, water-based coat

Oil-based varnish tinted with raw umber

Antique colored wax

you are in doubt, ask the advice of the store in which you bought the varnish.

The placemats demonstrate the different kinds of crackle varnish and illustrate the effects that can be achieved with each kind (see pages 10-14).

CRACKLE GLAZE

Use crackle glaze between two different colors of latex paint to produce a cracked or crazed second color, through which the underlying color can be seen. This is available in art stores.

WAX

Ordinary furniture wax can be used to give a polished sheen to an object that has been finished with flat varnish. Apply it with a damp cloth, and get into the habit of polishing the object every time you walk past it so that you not only have a beautifully gleaming finish but also have that lingering scent that only wax polish gives to a room.

ANTIQUING GLAZE

Use this when you want to produce really beautiful objects. As you gain experience and confidence, you may want to make your own glaze with mineral spirits and artists' oil paint. Mix them to a creamy consistency in a small glass jar and

apply the glaze with a soft cloth to give a soft "aged" appearance.

SANDING

You will need a selection of sandpapers, ranging from coarse to the finest you can buy. Not only must you prepare the surface of the object to be decorated, but finishing the decoupaged article with very fine sandpaper gives a smooth, professional-looking finish.

BRUSHES

In order to complete the projects shown in this book, you will need a selection of brushes. Good brushes are expensive, but as long as you look after them well, they will last far longer than less expensive brushes. However, there may be times when it it more convenient to use a cheaper brush, which you can discard when it is unusable.

After applying latex paint, wash your brushes thoroughly in water and detergent. It is a good idea to have separate brushes for oil paints and varnishes. Clean them with mineral spirits or a commercial cleaner.

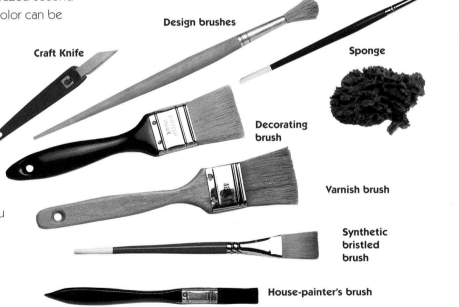

Design brushes

Craft Knife

Sponge

Decorating brush

Varnish brush

Synthetic bristled brush

House-painter's brush

VARNISH BRUSHES

These flat brushes can be synthetic or pure bristle. They are available in different widths. When you are using water-based varnishes and paints, synthetic brushes tend to give better results because they give a better flow and do not leave brush marks..

If you use crackle varnish, use two separate varnish brushes and label them for the appropriate stages because it is important that the two varnishes are not mixed when they are wet or the crackle will not work. Always clean the brushes immediately after use.

DECORATING BRUSHES

Look out for a variety of widths in hardware stores. If possible, choose the more expensive brushes, which do not shed hairs as much as cheaper ones. It can be extremely annoying to find that you have not noticed a stray hair until the paint or varnish has dried.

Use cheap brushes for shellac because denatured alcohol tends to ruin them. Do not use mineral spirits to clean brushes used for shellac.

WATERCOLOR BRUSHES

Use artists' paintbrushes to add fine details and for touching up. You will find a choice of widths and qualities in art stores, and the most useful for acrylic paints are sizes no. 4, no. 6, and no. 9. I used a flat-edged oil paintbrush for the edges of the table mats because it is easy to control.

ADDITIONAL EQUIPMENT

In addition to the above, you will need one or two other items to complete the projects.

SPONGES

Natural sponges produce the best and softest effects when you are sponging on paints, but if you use a synthetic sponge, tear rather than cut off small pieces so that they have slightly rough edges. All types of sponges are available in art stores.

ROLLER

A small rubber roller (sometimes called a brayer) or a small plastic roller of the kind sold in hardware stores for smoothing the edges of wallpaper is useful for pressing over glued images to remove all air bubbles and to give even adhesion. You can use the back of a spoon instead in small areas, and

when you are applying motifs to large, flat surfaces, such as furniture, you may be able to use your pastry rolling-pin. Press down with a firm, smooth motion, pushing air bubbles and excess glue from the center to the edges of the motif. Do not use your fingers, or you will tear the paper.

If the surface to which you are applying a motif

is uneven, use a slightly dampened sponge, pressed evenly from the center outward.

CLEANING MATERIALS

Use denatured alcohol to dilute shellac and button polish and to clean the brushes with which you apply these substances.

Mineral spirits can be used to clean the surface of an object before decoupage motifs are applied. Use it also to dilute oil-based paints and varnishes and to clean brushes.

Clean brushes used for latex paint and water-based varnishes with detergent and water. Work a small amount of undiluted detergent into the bristles first, then rinse them thoroughly with clean water.

TECHNIQUES

Decoupage is a very simple craft, and once you have mastered the few simple rules, you will be able to apply them to complicated projects. One of the most important rules, however, is to prepare the surface carefully and thoroughly before you even begin to think about the motifs you are going to use.

PREPARING SURFACES

NEW WOOD

Seal new wood with an acrylic primer/undercoat or with a shellac sanding sealer. Then apply a coat of latex or oil-based paint. If you prefer, stain the wood before sealing with a colored wood stain.

VARNISHED WOOD

Use medium-grit sandpaper to rub down the surface to provide a key to which the paint can adhere. You must make sure that you remove all flaking and loose varnish with sandpaper. If the sanding exposes bare wood, apply a primer/undercoat or a layer of shellac before painting.

PAINTED WOOD

If an article has been previously painted with a water-based paint, it can generally be painted over quite easily with either oil- or water-based paint. It must be well sanded, using medium sandpaper, working down to fine grit, to provide a key for an acrylic primer undercoat. If you are re-painting wood that has been previously painted with oil-based paint, it may have dried out enough over the years for you simply to apply latex paint after sanding it down lightly to provide a key. This can be done to achieve a distressed effect by sanding to reveal the old paint beneath.

MEDIUM DENSITY FIBERBOARD (MDF)

MDF is available from large lumber stores and most hardware stores, which will often cut it to the size you need. Treat it exactly as you would ordinary, untreated wood.

METAL

Use a wire brush to remove loose rust, and paint on a rust inhibitor such as red oxide (available from automobile parts suppliers) if the rust is deeply ingrained. You must apply a base coat of metal primer; if you do not, the metal will stain through any top coat of metal or oil-based paint you use.

CERAMICS

Lightly sand the surface to create a key, then simply apply a coat of acrylic primer/undercoat.

SEALING PAPER PRINTS

Always coat both sides of gift-wrap paper or photocopies with shellac. This not only protects the paper from the adhesive and varnish (which will cause the image to discolor), but also strengthens the paper and makes it easier to cut out. Use denatured alcohol to clean your brush.

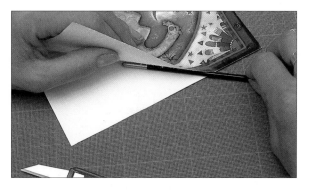

SEPARATING PICTURES

Most of us have kept greeting cards that we are reluctant to throw away, but are not sure what to do with. Decoupage could be the answer. The images are, however, usually printed on cardboard, and because the aim of decoupage is to lose the edges of the paper and "sink" the image in coats of varnish until it appears to be part of the original article, the picture needs to be separated from the cardboard backing.

Paint the picture side of the card with a coat of shellac. Carefully insert a craft knife between the picture and the card, making sure that the picture has a reasonable backing. It will be more difficult to separate if it is too thin. Peel back the picture from the card, working slowly and carefully, and use a paintbrush or ruler to hold the card as you gently lift the picture from its backing. When you have separated the picture, apply a coat of shellac to the back of the image to protect and thicken it.

PLACE MATS

These mats illustrate the different kinds of crackle varnish that can be applied and the different results that can be achieved. The motifs appear on page 46.

You will need
◊ pieces of MDF, each 10 x 12 inches
◊ acrylic primer/undercoat
◊ fine sandpaper
◊ latex paint (we used cream for the background and maroon for the edging line)
◊ decorating brush
◊ flat-edged, stiff-bristled paintbrush
◊ photocopied motifs
◊ watercolor paints (light brown, maroon, and green for color washing the motifs)
◊ watercolor brush
◊ hairdryer
◊ shellac
◊ nail scissors
◊ craft knife or scalpel
◊ craft glue
◊ sponge or roller
◊ crackle varnish (see below)
◊ artists' oil paint (raw umber)
◊ oil-based varnish (gloss or satin finish)

1 Seal the wood with acrylic primer/undercoat. When the primer is dry, apply two coats of cream-colored latex paint, allowing the first coat to dry thoroughly and sanding lightly before applying the second coat.

2 Use the flat-edged paintbrush to paint a maroon line around the edge of each mat. Leave to dry.

3 Age the photocopied motifs by covering the whole image with watered-down dark gold or light brown (use tea if you prefer). Make sure that you do not allow the motif to become too wet and mop up any excess liquid with paper towels.

4 When the background is dry, color the knights' cloaks (we used red, but you could use green), but do not use too strong a color or you will not get the "aged" effect. Use a hairdryer to speed up the drying process.

5 When the paint is dry, apply a coat of shellac or white button polish to the back and front of the paper. Use a hairdryer for speed.

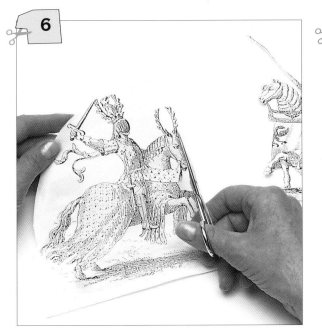

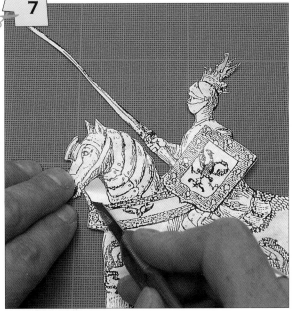

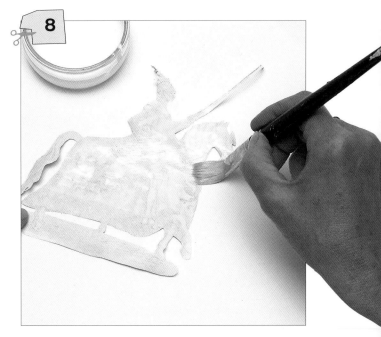

6 When the shellac is completely dry, cut neatly around the image with sharp nail scissors.

7 Use a craft knife or scalpel to cut out the intricate shapes, then place the motif on the mat, lightly marking the position with a pencil.

8 Apply a fine layer of white glue to the back of the motif, working from the center out to cover the shape evenly.

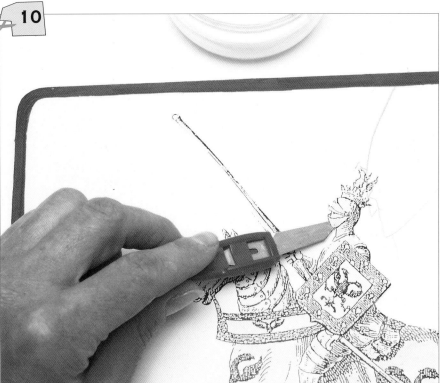

9 Place the motif on the mat, making sure it is correctly positioned, and press it down firmly with a damp sponge or roller.

10 Allow to dry, then check for air bubbles and lifting edges. Air bubbles in the center can be pierced and cut with the point of your craft knife, which can then be used to insert a tiny amount of glue. Use the point of your craft knife to add minute amounts of glue under any lifting edges. Press them down firmly but gently.

APPLYING CRACKLE VARNISH

This kind of varnish is used to give an interesting "antique" effect. The cracks can be large or small, but they are rarely consistent, which makes it almost impossible to produce two identical items. This inconsistency and unpredictability does help to give a feeling of age and authenticity to objects, and we have used the placemats to illustrate the differences between oil-based crackle (cracklure) and water-based crackle varnishes.

You will need

◊ two-stage oil-based or water-based crackle varnish
◊ varnishing brushes
◊ hairdryer (optional)
◊ artists' oil paint (raw umber)
◊ mineral spirits
◊ varnish
◊ fine sandpaper

TIP
• Hold the items you are varnishing up to the light to check that you have completely covered the surface and have not missed any small patches. Holding the object to the light will also help you see the crackles, which can be difficult to detect until you have worked over the surface with artists' oil paint.

WATER-BASED VARNISH

OIL-BASED VARNISH

OIL-BASED CRACKLE VARNISH

Cracklure or oil-based crackle varnish is affected by the atmosphere because the second coat is water-based and therefore absorbs moisture. If the second-stage crackle effect is not to your liking, you can simply wash it off and start again without damaging the paint and decoupage below the original first coat.

1 Use a flat varnishing brush to apply the first, oil-based crackle. Apply the varnish sparingly, beginning in the center and spreading it out before reloading the brush.

2 Leave the varnish to dry. This can take between 1 and 2 hours, depending on the humidity in the atmosphere. When the varnish is ready for the second stage, it feels smooth and dry when stroked, but tacky when gently touched with the fingertips.

3 Use a well-cleaned brush or a different one to apply the second coat of water-based varnish. Make sure you cover the entire surface and brush it in so that it adheres well to the first coat. Leave to dry for at least 1–4 hours, but preferably overnight. The cracks will begin to appear as soon as the varnish begins to dry, but they will not be visible unless you hold it to the light. Using a hairdryer, set on medium and held at a distance from the surface of the varnish, will encourage cracks to appear.

4 Squeeze about ¾ inch of artists' oil paint into a dish and add a small amount of mineral spirits to soften the paint. Use a soft cloth or paper towel to spread paint all over the surface of the varnish. Wipe off the excess paint with a clean cloth, leaving the crackle-effect enhanced by the darker oil paint.

5 Leave to dry for about 24 hours, then apply three or four coats of varnish, allowing the varnish to dry between coats and sanding each coat gently. Gloss varnish is hard-wearing and effective for table mats, and you might find a heat-resistant varnish in your local hardware store.

WATER-BASED CRACKLE VARNISH

If you buy this two-stage varnish from an art-supply store, you should be able to choose between large or small cracks. This kind of varnish is easy to use, and the results are always good. Although the cracks tend to look fairly predictable, you can achieve a good aging effect by rubbing artists' oil paint over the surface.

1 The first stage is a milky white fluid, which takes about 20 minutes to dry, when it becomes clear. If you want small cracks, apply a second coat of the stage-one fluid, which should be left to dry for a further 20 minutes.

2 When the stage one varnish is dry, apply the second stage. Make sure that the base coat is completely covered. Check by holding your work up to the light. Leave to dry for 20 minutes, and when the second stage is completely dry, cracks will have appeared over the whole surface.

3 Use a soft cloth, dampened with mineral spirits, to rub artists' oil paint over the surface of the varnish. Leave this to dry, which can take up to 24 hours.

4 Apply four coats of gloss, heat-proof polyurethane varnish, sanding with fine sandpaper between each coat.

CERAMIC LAMP

The base of this lamp was bought in a garage sale, but you can find similar plain bases in most department and home furnishing stores. This kind of lamp is suitable for Victorian animal illustrations – we used lizards, which we enlarged on a photocopier and color-washed.

You will need
◊ ceramic lamp base
◊ medium and fine sandpaper
◊ latex paint (yellow)
◊ decorating brushes for latex paint and varnish
◊ photocopied motifs
◊ watercolor paint (olive green)
◊ scissors and craft knife
◊ white glue
◊ sponge
◊ oil-based crackle varnish
◊ hairdryer (optional)
◊ artists' oil paint (raw umber)
◊ mineral spirits
◊ polyurethane varnish (satin finish)

TIP

• When you have used oil-based crackle varnish, you must finish off with oil-based varnish. Alternatively, use a layer of shellac between the crackle varnish and the acrylic varnish.

1 Rub over the lamp base gently with sandpaper to provide a key for the paint, then apply two coats of latex paint.

2 While the paint is drying, apply olive green watercolor to the lizards. Use the paint thinly to give an aged appearance. When the paint is dry, apply shellac to both sides of the motifs and leave to dry before you cut them out.

3 Use craft glue to stick the lizards to the base of the lamp. Press the motifs down firmly and evenly on the surface of the lamp and wipe away the excess glue.

4 When the glue is dry, apply the first stage of the crackle varnish. Leave it to dry until it feels smooth when stroked but sticky to the touch.

5 Apply the second stage of the crackle varnish, making sure that the whole surface is covered.

6 Leave the lamp to dry. This will depend on the temperature and humidity of the room in which you are working, but after a couple of hours you can use a hairdryer to encourage the crackles to form.

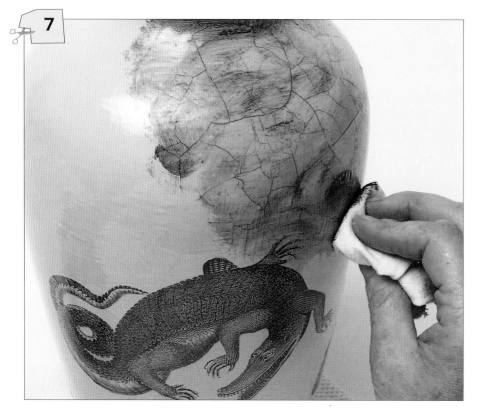

TIP

• Always clean away any glue from around the motifs because it will show up as lighter patches on the finished object if you apply crackle varnish over it.

7 Mix some artists' oil paint with mineral spirits and apply it to the surface of the lamp with a cloth.

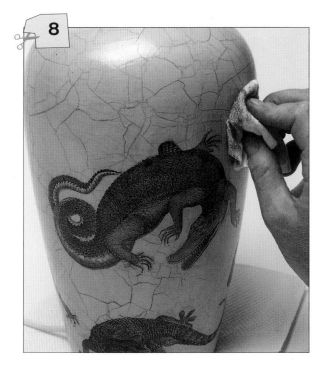

8 Rub the mixture into the cracks with a circular movement and remove the excess with a clean cloth. Leave to dry for about 2 hours.

9 Apply four or five coats of satin-finish varnish to "lose" the edges of the paper. A polyurethane varnish gives a slightly translucent finish, which is appropriate for a lamp. Finally, paint the shade with dark green latex paint to match the green of the lizards.

LETTER RACK

This letter rack was bought in a furniture warehouse, and it was decorated to be given as a wedding present. The motifs were photocopied from a log of the tour of the British Empire made by King George V and Queen Mary in 1901. The design was finished off with some stamps from the same period.

You will need

◊ letter rack
◊ shellac
◊ brush for shellac
◊ latex paint (petrol blue)
◊ 1-inch decorating brush
◊ photocopied motifs, stamps, and letters
◊ watercolor paint
◊ scissors and craft knife
◊ craft glue
◊ sponge and roller
◊ watercolor brush
◊ acrylic paint (gold)
◊ polyurethane varnish (satin finish)
◊ fine sandpaper
◊ fine steel wool

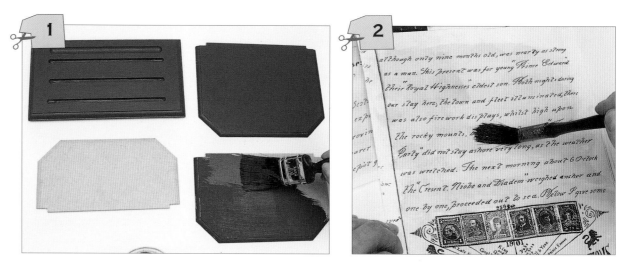

1 Seal the letter rack with shellac and, when it is dry, apply two coats of latex paint.

2 While the paint is drying, color wash the photocopies with light brown watercolor paint to give an aged appearance. Make sure the paper does not get too wet, or it will stretch and buckle. When it is dry, paint both sides of all the motifs with shellac.

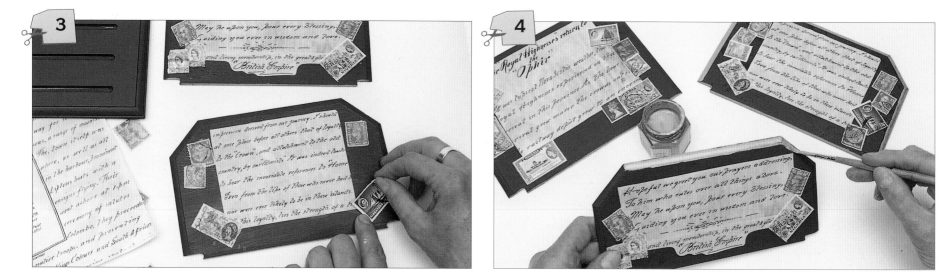

3 Cut out the motifs and use craft glue to stick them to the letter rack.

4 Use a fine paintbrush to apply gold acrylic paint to the edges of the letter rack.

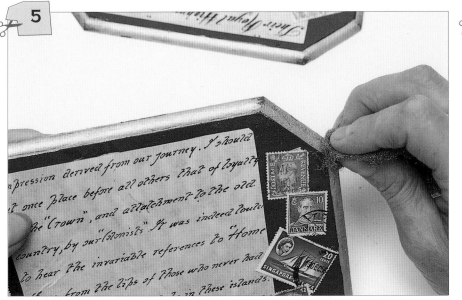

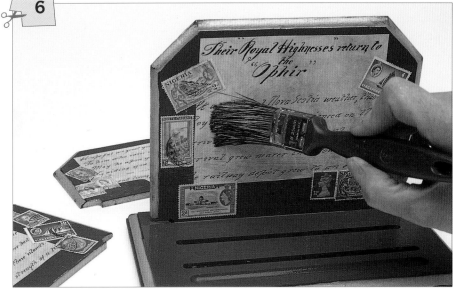

5 When the gold paint is dry, rub the corners with fine steel wool to achieve an aged effect.

6 Apply four coats of satin-finish polyurethane varnish, sanding lightly between each coat.

TIP

• Make a pencil holder for your desk from a cylindrical cardboard container or even an old tin can. This is an ideal way of using up those greeting cards that you don't want to throw away because you will need only one or two images. See page 9 for advice on separating the picture from thick cardboard.

FABRIC LAMPSHADE

Lampshades are available in such a wide choice of styles, sizes, and shapes that you are sure to find one you like. We used an old one, but a new, fabric-covered shade would do just as well. You can use any kind of motif – teddy bears for a child's room, for example, or cherubs for a guest room – and this was so easy to do that we decorated an old tray to match.

You will need
◊ lampshade
◊ craft glue
◊ 1-inch decorating brush
◊ latex paint (midnight blue)
◊ brushes for applying latex, watercolor and acrylic paints, and varnish
◊ photocopied motifs
◊ watercolor paint (pink)
◊ artists' acrylic paint (gold)
◊ scissors and craft knife
◊ varnish

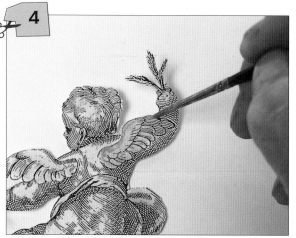

1 If you are using a fabric lampshade, apply a coat of craft glue, diluted to the consistency of paint, to bond the material and give a smooth surface to work on. Craft glue will not be affected by the heat of a 60w light bulb.

2 When the craft glue is dry, apply two coats of latex paint.

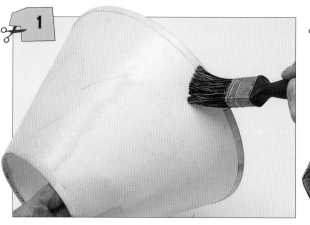

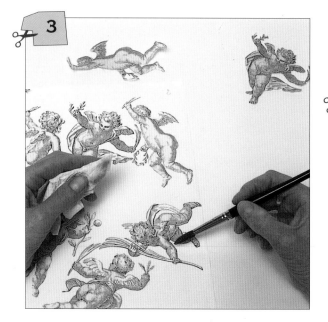

3 Paint the angels with watered-down pink watercolor.

4 Use a fine brush to add highlights to the angels with gold acrylic paint.

5 When the angels are quite dry, apply a coat of shellac to both sides of each one.

6

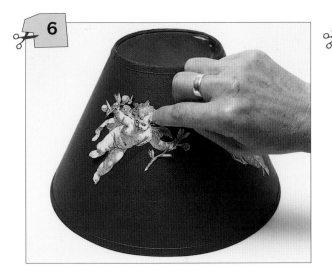

6 Cut out and glue the angels in position around the lampshade.

TIP

• When you are gluing motifs to curved surfaces, make small snips around the edges at intervals of about 1 inch to help make sure that the motifs lie perfectly flat.

8

8 When the glue is dry, apply at least five coats of varnish so that the edges of the paper are "lost."

7

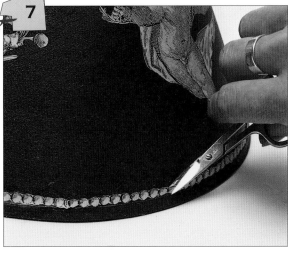

7 Add the edging to the top and bottom of the shade, snipping at 1-inch intervals to make sure it lies flat.

TRAY

An old tray was very quickly given a new lease of life with an undercoat of acrylic paint followed by two coats of midnight blue latex paint. When the paint was dry, cherubs like those used on the lampshade, were glued on with craft glue. When the glue was dry, a coat of flat varnish was applied.

We then used a water-based crackle varnish to create small cracks over the surface of the tray (see page 13). After painting on the first stage and allowing 20 minutes' drying time, the second-stage coat was added. The cracks began to show after about 20 minutes when the tray was held to the light. A little raw umber artists' oil paint was rubbed in, the tray was left to dry overnight, then four coats of gloss polyurethane varnish were applied

METAL TRUNK

This old metal trunk had been stored in a garage for years. It had seen better days, when it was used by an aunt to ship her possessions back and forth to Africa. There was a small area of rust, which was easily removed, then turning the trunk into a useful storage space that doubles as a coffee table was a straightforward matter.

You will need
◊ metal trunk
◊ medium and fine sandpaper
◊ rust remover
◊ inexpensive brushes for rust remover, iron oxide paint, and shellac
◊ iron oxide, rust-resistant paint
◊ mineral spirits
◊ primer/undercoat
◊ latex paints
◊ decorating brushes for paint and varnish
◊ gift-wrap paper with appropriate motifs
◊ shellac
◊ denatured alcohol
◊ scissors and craft knife
◊ masking tape
◊ craft glue
◊ sponge or roller
◊ polyurethane varnish (flat)
◊ artists' oil paint (raw umber)
◊ wax polish

1 Wash the trunk to remove all dirt and grease, then dry carefully. Rub away any loose paint or rust with medium sandpaper, brushing away all dust with a soft, dry brush. Apply rust remover to any areas affected by rust, remembering to treat the inside of the trunk as well. As you apply the rust remover, white appears on the affected areas. Apply further coats until no more white appears.

2 Paint the trunk, inside and out, with red oxide rust-resistant paint. Clean your brush thoroughly in mineral spirits.

3 Paint the trunk with primer/undercoat. When the primer is dry, apply two coats of latex paint. Apply the coats in opposite directions – cross-hatching – to give a surface that has an old, rough appearance, rather like linen.

TIP

• Always take time to remove all traces of rust. It can be heartbreaking to work hard to produce a beautifully decoupaged piece, only to have it completely spoiled, when rust stains break through.

4 Use a narrower brush to pick out the handles and edging strips in a contrasting color.

TIP

• When you use gift-wrap paper for motifs, always prepare two sheets, just in case you inadvertently tear the paper or make a mistake.

5 Apply shellac to both sides of the gift-wrap paper and clean your brush in denatured alcohol. When the shellac is dry, carefully cut out the motifs you want.

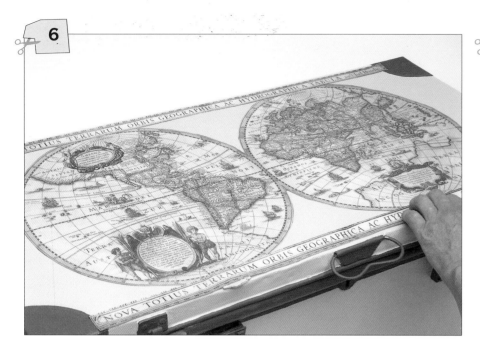

6 Arrange the motifs on the trunk, using masking tape to hold them in place until you are satisfied with their position. Mark the positions lightly with pencil. Remove the tape and apply an even coat of craft glue to the back of the motifs, pressing them down with a sponge or roller. When the glue is dry, apply a coat of flat polyurethane varnish to prevent too much oil paint from accumulating around the edges of the decoupage.

7 Use a soft cloth to apply a mixture of artists' oil paint and mineral spirits unevenly over the surface of the trunk. For example, we made the edges and corners darker and applied more oil paint around the locks and other areas where a well-traveled trunk would be expected to gather dust. Leave to dry overnight before applying three or four further coats of varnish, leaving each coat to dry and sanding it lightly with fine sandpaper between coats. Finally, build up several layers of wax polish to create a deep, lustrous sheen.

KEY BOX

This unpainted key box was found, almost by accident, in a furniture store. It is worth looking in department or craft stores, which often stock inexpensive, unpainted shelves and small cupboards that are ideal subjects for decoupage.

You will need

◊ unpainted wooden key box
◊ fine sandpaper
◊ mineral spirits
◊ shellac or acrylic primer/undercoat
◊ brushes for shellac, varnish (you will need two), and latex and watercolor paints
◊ latex paint (rust, blue, and two shades of cream)
◊ wax candle
◊ photocopied coat of arms and keys
◊ watercolor paints
◊ hairdryer (optional)
◊ scissors and craft knife
◊ craft glue
◊ sponge or roller
◊ fine steel wool
◊ water-based crackle varnish
◊ artists' oil paint (raw umber)
◊ oil-based varnish (flat)

1 Gently sand the surface of the box with fine sandpaper.

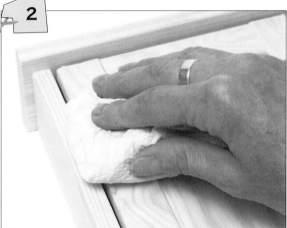

2 Use mineral spirits on a clean cloth to remove any dust and grease from the surface of the wood, then seal the box. We used shellac sanding sealer rather than white primer so that the grain of the wood showed through to give a distressed effect when the box was sanded.

3 Paint the outer panels, the top and bottom, and inside the box with two coats of rust red or brick red latex paint.

4 Give the front panel two coats of cream-colored latex paint. Making the first coat slightly darker than the second and allowing it to show through streaks in the second coat will help give depth to a flat surface.

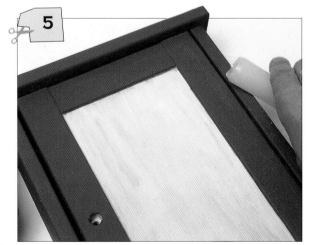

5 When the paint is dry, rub the areas you would like to look distressed with a wax candle. The usual places are near the knob and on the edges of the door, and the wax makes it easier to remove the contrasting color with steel wool.

6 Paint the door frame with blue latex paint.

7 While the paint dries, color the motifs. Use a hairdryer to speed up the drying process if you wish.

8 When the motifs are dry, cut them out and apply shellac to the front and back.

9 Apply craft glue evenly to the back of the motifs and place them on the front of the central panel, pressing them down firmly and carefully with a damp sponge or roller.

10 When the glue is dry, use fine steel wool to distress the areas you have previously rubbed with the candle wax. Remove all traces of dust with a dry paint brush.

11 Apply the first stage of the crackle varnish and leave to dry for about 20 minutes.

12 Apply the second stage of the crackle varnish, then leave it to dry thoroughly.

13 Rub artists' oil paint into the cracks with a soft cloth dampened with mineral spirits. Wipe away any excess paint.

14 Leave overnight for the paint to dry; then apply two or three coats of flat varnish.

WOODEN BOX

These round wooden boxes are sold in some large furniture stores, and
they are sometimes sold by mail order, so it is worth looking in hobby and craft magazines.
They are not expensive and are available in a variety of sizes, so they are ideal for
personalizing to give as a gift.

You will need
◊ wooden box
◊ shellac
◊ latex paint (black)
◊ brushes for applying shellac, latex, and
  watercolor paints and varnish
◊ photocopied motifs
◊ watercolor paint
◊ masking tape
◊ craft glue
◊ gift-wrap tape (optional)
◊ acrylic varnish

1 Seal the surface of the box with a coat of shellac. When it is dry, apply a coat of black latex paint, which will dry to charcoal gray.

2 While the box dries, paint the photocopied motifs with watercolors. We used lions from an old history book and painted them yellow. When the paint is dry, apply shellac to both sides of each motif.

3 Arrange the motifs around the side of the box, using masking tape to hold them in place. When you are satisfied with the arrangement, remove the tape and glue the motifs in place with craft glue.

4 If you wish, decorate the rim of the box lid with a strip of narrow gift-wrap tape.

5 When the glue is dry, apply at least five coats of quick-drying acrylic varnish.

WATERING CAN

These watering cans are sold in hardware stores and garden centers. If you are careful, you can use the can after you have decorated it. You must protect the decoupage with many coats of varnish and be careful when you fill the can that you do not hit it against the faucet and chip the varnish.

You will need
◊ galvanized iron watering can
◊ vinegar
◊ iron oxide, rust-resistant paint
◊ inexpensive decorating
   brushes for rust-resistant paint
   and shellac
◊ latex paint (pale blue)
◊ decorating brush
◊ gift-wrap paper or suitable
   motifs
◊ shellac
◊ scissors and craft knife
◊ masking tape
◊ craft glue
◊ sponge or roller
◊ watercolor brush
◊ acrylic paints
◊ artists' oil paint (raw umber)
◊ mineral spirits
◊ quick-drying varnish
◊ polyurethane (gloss)

1 Carefully wipe the metal with a solution of one part vinegar to one part water to remove all traces of grease. If your watering can is an old one, clean it as shown for the the trunk (see page 22).

2 Apply a coat of red oxide, rust-resistant paint to the watering can. Use an inexpensive brush.

3 When the rust-resistant paint is dry, apply two coats of latex paint. Leave to dry.

4 While the paint dries, prepare the motifs by applying shellac to both sides. When the shellac is dry, carefully cut out the motifs.

5 Arrange the motifs on the watering can, holding them in place with small pieces of masking tape until you are satisfied with their position. Mark their positions lightly with a pencil. Remove the tape and glue the motifs in position with craft glue. Press them down carefully and evenly with a damp sponge or small roller.

6 While the glue is drying, use a watercolor brush to paint the edges of the can. Use tubes of artists' acrylic paint, which are ideal for small areas.

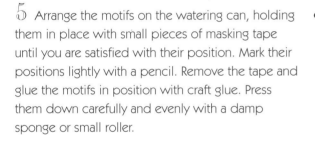

TIP

• You will find a small number of acrylic paints useful because you can mix the colors with white latex paint to make a choice of colors that can be used for touching up images, highlighting edges, or painting lines.

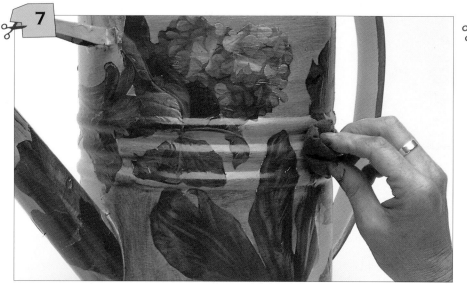

7 When the adhesive and paint are completely dry, mix a small amount of raw umber with mineral spirits and use a clean cloth to rub it over the surface of the can to "age" the surface. Add extra antique glaze to areas that you would expect to accumulate dirt over the years.

8 Apply at least four coats of a quick-drying varnish to "lose" the edges of the motifs. Give a final coat of hard-gloss polyurethane. If you want to use the can, you will need to apply at least five coats of varnish to seal and protect it. Handle the finished can carefully so that no water gets under the surface of the varnish.

PAINTED TABLE WITH CRACKLE EFFECT

Once you have started to use decoupage to transform old furniture, nothing will escape your attention. This old table had stood outside for many years, but it needed only sanding to remove the surface and remains of the old varnish and to provide a key for the undercoat before it was ready to be decorated for its new life.

You will need
◊ small wooden table
◊ medium and fine sandpaper
◊ acrylic primer/undercoat
◊ decorating brushes for primer/undercoat, crackle glaze, and latex paint
◊ latex paint (mauve and yellow)
◊ crackle glaze
◊ flat-edged brush
◊ gift-wrap paper or suitable motifs
◊ shellac
◊ scissors and craft knife
◊ masking tape
◊ craft glue
◊ sponge or roller
◊ quick-drying acrylic varnish

1 Prepare the surface of the table by sanding it with medium, then fine, sandpaper. Brush away any dust and apply a coat of acrylic primer.

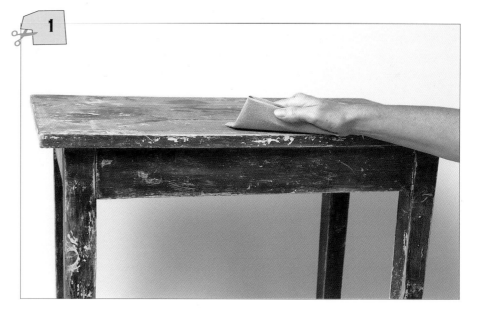

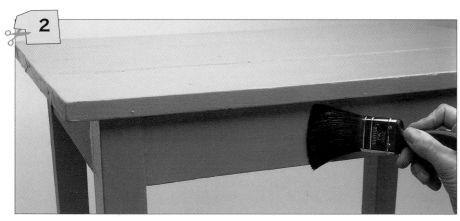

2 Paint the surface of the table with latex paint. Choose a color that you want to show through the cracks in the glaze. When the paint is dry, apply a coat of crackle glaze.

3 When the glaze is dry – after about 30 minutes – apply the second coat of latex paint. Load your brush well and cover the surface of the table in one movement. If you apply two coats, the crackle effect will not work. As the paint dries, you will see the cracks appearing.

4

 Use a flat-edged brush to highlight the edges of the table with the first color of latex paint.

> ### TIP
>
> • Apply as many coats of varnish as necessary to "sink" the edges of the motifs. When it is completely dry, it can be finished with a coat of oil-based satin varnish.

5

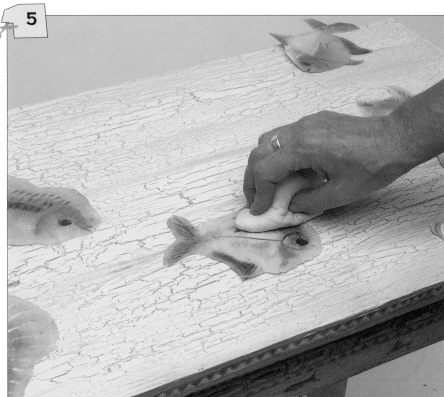

6

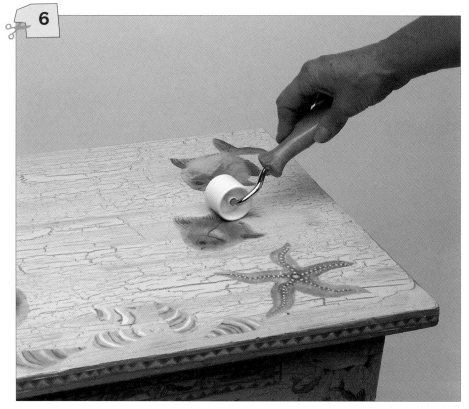

5 While the paint is drying, apply shellac to both sides of the motifs and, when it is dry, carefully cut out the motifs. Arrange the motifs over the table, holding them in place with masking tape until you are happy with the arrangement.

6 Use craft glue to glue the motifs in place, pressing them down with a damp sponge or roller. On a large area such as a table, you could even use a rolling pin.

7

8

7 Use a damp sponge to press the motifs into awkward corners.

8 When the adhesive is completely dry, apply four or five coats of a quick-drying acrylic varnish.

GALVANIZED IRON BUCKET

This old galvanized iron bucket was found in a dumpster, but it was such an unusual shape that we decided to give it a new life as a container for dried flowers. You could use a similar container in the kitchen to store bread. It needed a lot of work to remove patches of rust and to clean it up before it could be decorated.

You will need

◊ iron bucket
◊ medium and fine sandpaper
◊ rust remover
◊ inexpensive brushes for rust remover and iron oxide paint
◊ iron oxide, rust-resistant paint
◊ primer/undercoat (optional)
◊ crackle glaze
◊ 1¼-inch decorating brushes for glaze and paint
◊ latex paints (sea green and dark blue)
◊ gift-wrap paper or suitable motifs
◊ shellac
◊ scissors and craft knife
◊ removable adhesive tak (optional)
◊ craft glue
◊ sponge or roller
◊ artists' oil paint (raw umber)
◊ mineral spirits
◊ quick-drying varnish (flat)
◊ soil-based varnish (flat)
◊ wax polish

1 Remove as much dirt as you can with a stiff brush, then use medium sandpaper to remove patches of rust. Paint rust remover on all affected areas, continuing to apply the remover until it stops turning white. Remember to treat the inside and the lid. Paint the bucket inside and out with rust-resistant paint.

2 Because we wanted the color of the red oxide paint to show through the cracks, we left this as the base coat. If you prefer, apply a coat of primer in the color of your choice. When the base coat is dry, apply a coat of crackle glaze, making sure that you completely cover the surface of the bucket.

3 When the glaze is dry, apply a coat of latex paint. Use a well-loaded brush, but do not go over areas that have already been painted because this will prevent the cracking effect. As the second coat begins to dry, cracks will appear. Leave until it is quite dry.

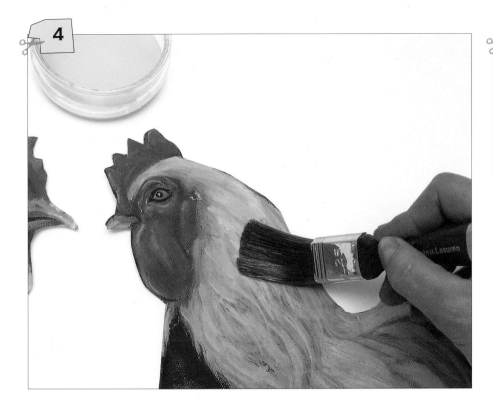

4 Apply shellac to both sides of the motifs or gift-wrap paper. The honey-colored shellac will have a slightly aging effect on the motifs.

5 Cut out the motifs when the shellac is dry and use craft glue to stick them to the sides of the bucket, using a damp sponge or roller to press them down evenly.

6 Use the point of your craft knife to check that all the edges are firmly stuck down, adding tiny amounts of glue if necessary. Remove air bubbles by making a small slit in the paper and inserting a little glue on your craft knife.

7 Soften a small amount of artists' oil paint in a little mineral spirits to make an antique glaze, and use a soft cloth to apply it all over the surface of the bucket.

TIP

• Crackle glaze, which is available from art supply stores, can be used to enhance the background for the decoupage. The glaze cracks the top coat of paint, allowing the color of the base coat to be seen through the cracks.

9 Apply five coats of a quick-drying varnish to "lose" the edges of the motifs. It is milky white when it is wet, but it dries clear.

8 Use a paintbrush to apply extra antique glaze in the areas you would expect dirt to accumulate. Dip your cloth in the glaze and add extra to the corners and edges.

TIP

• Applying antiquing glaze can be dirty work and cleaning your fingernails of dark oil paint can be difficult. Wear rubber gloves.

10 At this stage, you can stand back to admire your handiwork before you apply the final coats of varnish. We decided to add contrasting blue to the handle of the lid.

TIP
• Because there are so many different varnishes on the market, always read the manufacturer's instructions before you begin.

11 Apply a final coat of oil-based satin-finish varnish and, when it is dry, polish with wax to give a warm sheen to the finished bucket.

PAPER RACK

This old paper rack was transformed into a gift for a friend who was going to live in Paris. The antique-looking "French newspapers" were, in fact, photocopied from a decoupage source book – it is amazing just how many different kinds of image are being reproduced these days.

You will need
◊ paper rack
◊ fine and medium sandpaper
◊ mineral spirits
◊ brushes for primer, shellac, and gloss and watercolor paints
◊ acrylic primer/undercoat
◊ gloss paint (black)
◊ photocopied newspapers
◊ scissors
◊ watercolor paints
◊ paintbrushes
◊ shellac
◊ masking tape
◊ craft glue
◊ gloss varnish

1 Use medium sandpaper to sand the rack and then clean it with mineral spirits. Apply primer/undercoat and, when it is dry, apply a coat of black gloss paint. Leave to dry overnight.

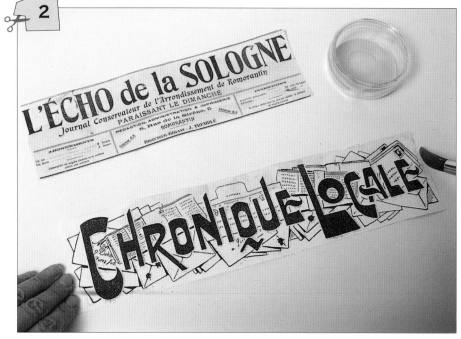

2 Cut out the newspaper photocopies and apply a wash of watercolor to age them.

3 When the paint is dry, apply shellac to both sides of each piece.

4

5

4 Arrange the motifs on the paper rack, holding them in position with small pieces of masking tape so that you can assess their positions. Remove the tape and glue the motifs in place with craft glue.

5 Leave the glue to dry before varnishing. You should apply at least five coats – more if you wish – sanding each coat lightly with fine sandpaper before applying the next.

TIP
• When you want a good black background, use black gloss paint. Black latex paint tends to dry to charcoal gray.

SMALL DESK

This pretty little chest was found in a thrift shop. It had been left out in the rain, which had lifted the veneer from the surface, revealing the underlying pine. It was such a perfect size and such a useful piece that it was impossible to resist decorating it.

You will need
◊ medium sandpaper
◊ mineral spirits
◊ acrylic primer/undercoat
◊ decorating brushes for primer/undercoat, crackle glaze, and latex paint (wide and narrow)
◊ gift-wrap paper or suitable motifs
◊ shellac
◊ latex paint (cream, petrol blue, and sand)
◊ natural sponge
◊ scissors and craft knife
◊ masking tape
◊ craft glue
◊ sponge or roller
◊ acrylic varnish
◊ oil-based crackle varnish (optional)
◊ oil-based varnish (satin finish)
◊ wax polish

1 Remove all old varnish and polish by sanding with medium sandpaper and wiping with mineral spirits.

2 Apply a coat of acrylic primer/undercoat. While the primer is drying, apply shellac to both sides of the motifs.

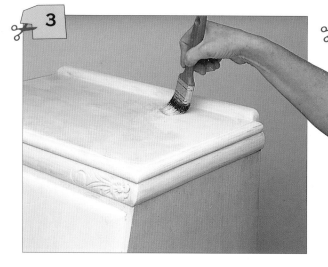

3 When the primer/undercoat is dry, paint the desk with the first coat of cream-colored latex paint.

4 Leave the latex paint to dry, then use the natural sponge to dab the blue and sand-colored paint over the cream undercoat. Dab the paint lightly, turning your wrist slightly to vary the pattern of sponging. If you do not like the result, you can wash off the paint before it dries or start again by repainting the cream base coat.

5 Use a narrow brush to pick out the edges of the desk with blue latex paint.

TIP

• Before you glue a large motif to a surface, make sure it has been thoroughly prepared with shellac. Not only will this help prevent it from stretching as you glue it in place, the shellac will help overcome the problem of air bubbles and creases.

8 Apply four or five coats of acrylic varnish to "lose" the edges of the motifs. When this is perfectly dry, follow with a coat of oil-based varnish or, if you prefer, crackle varnish (see page 12), before finishing off with an oil-based, satin-finish varnish and wax polish.

6 While the paint dries, cut out the motifs from the prepared gift-wrap paper and arrange them over the surface of the desk, holding them in place with masking tape until you are happy with the arrangement. Glue the motifs with craft glue, using a sponge or roller to make sure they are pressed down evenly and smoothly.

7 Use a craft knife to check that all the edges are firmly held down by glue. If necessary, apply a small amount of glue. Slit any air bubbles with your craft knife and insert tiny amounts of glue before pressing down the paper again.

WASTEPAPER BASKET

This wastebasket has been decorated with a collage of illustrations cut from comics and computer magazines. It was going to be placed in a boy's room, so he chose and cut out the images himself.

You will need

◊ metal wastepaper basket
◊ acrylic primer/undercoat
◊ latex paint (red)
◊ paint and varnishes brushes
◊ comics and magazines
◊ scissors and craft knife
◊ shellac
◊ craft glue
◊ quick-drying acrylic varnish
◊ acrylic varnish (gloss)

1 Paint the inside and outside of the wastebasket with acrylic primer, then apply two coats of latex paint so that a bright color will be visible if there are any gaps in the collage.

2 While the paint is drying, cut out the images from the magazines. Coat both sides of each one with shellac. You may find it easier to do this before cutting the shapes from the magazines.

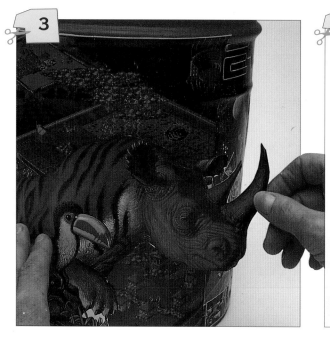

3 Beginning with the large, background pictures, use craft glue to stick the images over the surface of the wastebasket.

4 When the glue is completely dry, apply five coats of acrylic varnish, then finish with a coat of gloss varnish.

MOTIFS

10127 — CM

SUPPLIERS

UK

All About Art, 31 Sheen Road, Richmond Surrey, TW9 1AD

Varnishes, brushes, crackle glazes, decoupage source books. Any equipment needed and not in stock will be ordered. An excellent professional service is given by fully trained staff on all materials sold in the shop.

Craig & Rose Plc, 172 Leith Walk, Edinburgh EH6 5EB

Gold leaf, gold size, transparent oil glaze, extra pale dead flat varnish, quick-drying varnish (Mapfix). Nationwide stockists and paint manufacturers.

Belinda Ballantine, The Abbey Brewery, Malmesbury, Wiltshire SN16 9AS

For all decoupage materials

The Dover Bookshop, 18 Earlham Street, London WC2H 9LN

For decoupage print source books. Catalogue available on request.

Beaver Building Supplies, 300 Upper Richmond Road West, London SW14 7JG

Hardware DIY shop, with an enormous range of emulsion colours, who are happy to mix up 100ml small tins.

Hawkins & Co., St Margaret Halston, Norfolk IP20 0PJ

Mail order decoupage scraps.

USA

National Guild of Decoupageurs, 807 Rivard Boulevard, Grosse Pointe, MI 48230

If you write to the above address they will advise you about suppliers of decoupage equipment in your area.

Dew Enterprises, Don Woodegeard, 6232 Hickory Creek Road, High Point, NC 27263

Furniture, plant stands, drop-leaf coffee and end tables, and many more unfinished products for decoupage.

Dover Pictorial Archive Book Catalog, Dover Publications Inc., 31 East 2nd Street, Mineola, NY 11501

The world's largest collection of copyright-free illustrations and designs for artists, designers, and crafts people.

Plaid Enterprises Inc., PO Box 7600, Norcross, GA 30091–7600

Finishes, decoupage paste, antiquing varnishes, catalog supplied on request.

AUSTRALIA

Paper N'Things, 88 Union Street, Armadale, Victoria 3143

For all decoupage materials.

Oxford Art Supplies Pty Ltd, 221–223 Oxford Street, Darlinghurst, Sydney, N.S.W 2010

For general art supplies.

Janets Art Suppliers and Art Books, 145 Victoria Avenue, Chatsworth, Sydney, N.S.W. 2067

For decoupage kits, materials, papers and scraps and unfinished wooden items.

Art and Craft, 45 Targo Street, Bundaberg, Queensland 4670

For general art supplies.

Queensland Handicrafts, 6 Manning Street, South Brisbane, Queensland 4101

CANADA

Woolfits Art Enterprises Inc., 390 Dupont Street, Toronto, Ontario M5T 1V7

For information about decoupage suppliers.